Inside the NHL

Montreal Canadiens

Ramey Temple

www.av2books.com

AV² provides enriched content that supplements and complements this book. Weigl's AV² books strive to create inspired learning and engage young minds in a total learning experience.

Your AV² Media Enhanced books come alive with...

Audio
Listen to sections of the book read aloud.

Key Words
Study vocabulary, and complete a matching word activity.

Video
Watch informative video clips.

Quizzes
Test your knowledge.

Embedded Weblinks
Gain additional information for research.

Slide Show
View images and captions, and prepare a presentation.

Try This!
Complete activities and hands-on experiments.

... and much, much more!

Go to **www.av2books.com,** and enter this book's unique code.

BOOK CODE

Y 5 3 3 8 9 8

AV² by Weigl brings you media enhanced books that support active learning.

Published by AV² by Weigl
350 5ᵗʰ Avenue, 59ᵗʰ Floor
New York, NY 10118
Websites: www.av2books.com   www.weigl.com

Library of Congress Control Number: 2014951926

ISBN 978-1-4896-3152-7 (hardcover)
ISBN 978-1-4896-4016-1 (softcover)
ISBN 978-1-4896-3153-4 (single-user eBook)
ISBN 978-1-4896-3154-1 (multi-user eBook)

Printed in the United States of America in Brainerd, Minnesota
1 2 3 4 5 6 7 8 9 0   19 18 17 16 15

032015
WEP050315

Senior Editor Heather Kissock
Art Director Terry Paulhus

Photo Credits
Every reasonable effort has been made to trace ownership and to obtain permission to reprint copyright material. The publishers would be pleased to have any errors or omissions brought to their attention so that they may be corrected in subsequent printings.

Weigl acknowledges Getty Images and iStock as its primary image suppliers for this title.

Montreal Canadiens

CONTENTS

Introduction

The Montreal Canadiens began play in 1909, and are the oldest team in the National Hockey League (NHL). In fact, the Canadiens existed even before the NHL itself was founded in 1917. The Canadiens are the most celebrated hockey team in the world, not only for their 105-year **franchise** history, but because they have won the Stanley Cup a record 24 times, and reached the final 35 times. The French-Canadian audience is so large that games are broadcast in both French and English.

A Canadien since the 2008–2009 season, Max Pacioretty signed a six-year extension in 2012 to remain in Montreal and push for Stanley Cup number 25.

The "Habs" have not won the Cup since 1993, which also marks the last time a team from Canada was hockey's champion. Things are looking brighter for le Club de hockey Canadien, the team's official name. They captured a Northeast Division Championship in 2013, earning a second **seed** in the **playoffs**. They then skated all the way into the conference finals, where they lost to the Ottawa Senators in five games.

Carey Price was the winning goalie in an NHL best of 38 games during the 2010–2011 season.

Montreal
CANADIENS

Arena Bell Centre

Division Atlantic Division

Head Coach Michel Therrien

Location Montreal, Quebec, Canada

NHL Stanley Cup Titles 1916, 1924, 1930, 1931, 1944, 1946, 1953, 1956, 1957, 1958, 1959, 1960, 1965, 1966, 1968, 1969, 1971, 1973, 1976, 1977, 1978, 1979, 1986, 1993

Nicknames The Flying Frenchmen, the Habs

25 percent of all Stanley Cup titles

25 Prince of Wales Trophies

84 Playoff Appearances

History

During Jean Beliveau's 20 seasons as a Canadien, he hoisted the Stanley Cup 10 times. After he retired, he won the Cup another seven times as an executive. His 17 Stanley Cup victories are the most achieved by any individual in NHL history.

The Canadiens were founded in 1909 by J. Ambrose O'Brien as a part of the National Hockey Association (NHA), which was the main hockey group at the time. The Canadiens won their very first Stanley Cup in 1916, a year before the NHL was formed. Players were each awarded a generous bonus of $238 for the Cup victory in 1916.

In the long and storied history of the Canadiens, there have been 54 Hall of Fame players who proudly wore the classic "C" and "H" **logo** on the front of their jerseys. Despite so many legendary players, the Canadiens fell on hard times and nearly went out of business during the **Great Depression**. In fact, their rivals, the Montreal Maroons, were forced to shut down in 1939. Even during those dark years, the team kept winning. However, after they won their fourth Cup in 1931, they did not win another until 1944. At the time, this was the longest string of seasons the team had gone through without winning a Cup. The strong tradition of winning has made lifelong Canadien fans impatient for Cup number 25, after the team captured number 24 back in 1993, a streak of 21 years and counting without a Cup.

In 2009, Canadiens, past and present, gathered for a celebration of the franchise's 100-year history.

The Arena

The Bell Centre is home to the Montreal Canadiens and their fans, who always stand proudly during the Canadian national anthem.

The Canadiens have come a long way from tiny Jubilee Rink, their home ice rink during the 1909–1910 season, which seated only 3,000 fans. In the 104 seasons since, they have played in the Westmount Arena, the Jubilee Arena, the Mount Royal Arena, and for 70 magical seasons at the Montreal Forum, from 1926 to 1996.

In 1996, the Habs moved to the Bell Centre in Montreal, Quebec. Since that time, the Bell Centre has been one of the busiest arenas in Canada, hosting basketball, theater, and, of course, hockey. The Canadiens and their fans remain eager to host a Stanley Cup Final in their new building, which boasts the fifth-largest number of ticket sales for any Canadian arena.

Located in the middle of the bustling city of Montreal, the Bell Centre has the distinction of being the largest hockey arena in the world. It can seat up to 21,273 people. Inside the Bell Centre is one of the most popular sports restaurants in Montreal, La Cage aux Sports.

A statue of hockey great Maurice Richard has stood proudly in front of the Bell Centre since 2008.

Where They Play

Map labels:

CANADA
- British Columbia **7**
- Alberta **4** **3**
- Saskatchewan
- Manitoba **14**
- Ontario

UNITED STATES
- Washington
- Oregon
- Idaho
- Montana
- North Dakota
- Minnesota **11**
- Wisconsin
- Nevada **6**
- Utah
- Wyoming
- South Dakota
- Iowa **8**
- Illinois
- California **5**
- Colorado **9**
- Nebraska
- Kansas
- Missouri **13**
- Arizona **2** **1**
- New Mexico
- Oklahoma
- Arkansas
- Texas **10**
- Louisiana
- Miss[issippi]

Pacific Ocean

MEXICO

Gulf of Mexico

NHL WESTERN CONFERENCE

PACIFIC DIVISION

1	Anaheim Ducks	5	Los Angeles Kings
2	Arizona Coyotes	6	San Jose Sharks
3	Calgary Flames	7	Vancouver Canucks
4	Edmonton Oilers		

CENTRAL DIVISION

8	Chicago Blackhawks	12	Nashville Predators
9	Colorado Avalanche	13	St. Louis Blues
10	Dallas Stars	14	Winnipeg Jets
11	Minnesota Wild		

Centre Bell

Arena
Bell Centre, Montreal, Canada

Location
1909 Avenue des Canadiens-de-Montréal, Montreal, QC H4B 5G0

Broke Ground
June 22, 1993

Completed
March 16, 1996

Features
- three-tier layout with very steep grandstands to improve views
- live band stage
- personal scoreboards for sections that do not have views of the main scoreboard

LEGEND
☆ Bell Centre
■ Eastern Conference
■ Western Conference

ATLANTIC DIVISION
15 Boston Bruins	☆ 19 Montreal Canadiens
16 Buffalo Sabres	20 Ottawa Senators
17 Detroit Red Wings	21 Tampa Bay Lightning
18 Florida Panthers	22 Toronto Maple Leafs

METROPOLITAN DIVISION
23 Carolina Hurricanes	27 New York Rangers
24 Columbus Blue Jackets	28 Philadelphia Flyers
25 New Jersey Devils	29 Pittsburgh Penguins
26 New York Islanders	30 Washington Capitals

The Uniforms

The Montreal Canadiens have always had the initials 'CH' as their main logo. The letters represent the official team name, le Club de hockey Canadien.

The Canadiens went back to wearing their red jerseys at home in the 2003–2004 season. Red had been used as the away jersey color from 1970 through 2003.

HOME

The Canadiens have changed their uniforms many times since 1909, but have always kept the same three classic colors of blue, red, and white, to match the French flag. From 1917 through 1919, the Canadiens jersey featured a turtle neck, which came back again in 1924–1925, but was never seen again.

AWAY

The designs on the jerseys have all had small stripes along the sides and across the top, with at least 20 variations over the years. In the end, though, the uniform and logo have remained true to the original 1909 design. Players wear royal blue pants and blue or white helmets, depending on whether the game is played at home or on the road.

The blue stripe across the red jerseys has always existed. During a brief period from 1944 to 1947, the blue stripe also appeared on the white jerseys.

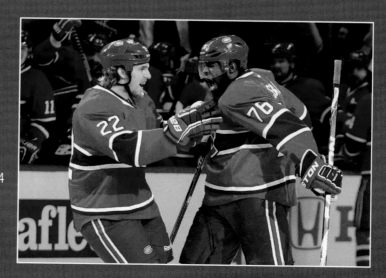

Helmets and Face Masks

The team logo was added to the helmets of all Canadiens position players in **2007.**

Carey Price is known for changing his mask design several times throughout a season.

Since the late 1970s, the NHL has made wearing helmets mandatory for all players. Position players for the Canadiens wear simple blue and white helmets that match their blue, red, and white jerseys. The Canadiens have had many goaltenders decorate their helmets in unique ways, a celebrated tradition in the modern NHL.

Canadiens goalies have been among the most creative in the league when it comes to helmet designs. David Aebischer wore one of the more famous goalie masks in Habs history. His mask featured the abominable snowman, a nod to his nickname, "Abby." Yann Danis, another creative Canadien goalie, put the Montreal cityscape on his helmet, with gray and black colors used for the buildings. Old-school Canadiens fans can still remember the simple mask that Ken Dryden wore, back when hockey masks only protected the face. This mask had blue and red circles, which looked something like a bulls-eye, aimed right at Dryden's eyes.

Although Canadien goaltenders have a variety of art on their helmets, they are all sure to include the famous "CH" logo in some way.

The Coaches

Ten different men have won the Stanley Cup while coaching the Canadiens.

Michel Therrien is the current head coach of the Canadiens. His team was within two victories of the Stanley Cup Final in 2014.

When a team plays 105 seasons and wins 24 championships, it is bound to produce a number of highly decorated coaches. The Canadiens have had 34 coaches, many of whom were previously players. Being a coach of a storied franchise like the Canadiens comes with a great deal of pressure, but also with great rewards.

TOE BLAKE Joseph Hector "Toe" Blake was the head coach of the Canadiens for 13 seasons. During that time, Blake helped the team win eight Stanley Cups, after having already won two as a player. On the ice, Blake was an accomplished left wing known as the "Old Lamplighter." On the bench, players took to calling him "Toe," and the nickname stuck.

SCOTTY BOWMAN Scotty Bowman has won nine Stanley Cups as a head coach, five of which he won with the Canadiens in just eight seasons. He currently holds the NHL record for most wins in league history, with 1,244. Bowman won a record 60 games in the 1976–1977 season. This win total broke the record he had set a year earlier with the Canadiens when the team won 58 games.

MICHEL THERRIEN Michel Therrien is the current coach of the Canadiens. He is a former NHL scout and former head coach of the Pittsburgh Penguins. Therrien, whose tenacity earned him the nickname "Bulldog," was also the coach of the Canadiens for three seasons, more than a decade before he returned to the bench in Montreal in 2012.

Fans and the Internet

Nearly 1 million Canadiens fans packed the Bell Centre during the 2013–2014 season. These excited fans chanted and cheered, while often dressed in head-to-toe Habs gear.

Laf

Canadiens fans can be seen all over Montreal with blue and red stripes painted on their faces and waving the "CH" flags proudly. The team also has several blogs for fans in search of more news, and an online community where they can voice their opinions about the game and the players. Among the more popular Canadiens blogs are Eyes on the Prize and HabsAddict.com.

There is also plenty of news and information on the official Canadiens de Montreal NHL website, where the home page has been split so that the entire website can be accessed in either French or English. The site boasts a fan countdown for the start of the new season, the team's schedule, tickets, a team store, and even a place for fans to create their own Canadiens **avatar.**

Signs
of a fan

#1 Canadiens fans often go to great lengths to earn the chance to buy playoff tickets for Habs games. In some cases, this means sleeping outside the arena overnight.

#2 Many Habs fans join their favorite Canadiens players in growing playoff beards.

Legends of the Past

Many great players have suited up for the Canadiens. A few of them have become icons of the team and the city it represents.

Guy Lafleur

Guy Lafleur was a key contributor to the Canadiens on six different Stanley Cup Championship teams. He was often described as "smooth" for the way he would glide on the ice effortlessly and make the game of hockey look easy. Lafleur won his first Cup in 1973, and during the most impressive six-year stretch of his career, from 1974 to 1980, he played in six All-Star games, won the Hart Memorial Trophy as the league's most valuable player (MVP) twice, never scored fewer than 119 points, and won the Stanley Cup in four consecutive seasons. Lafleur still holds a slew of Canadiens career records, including most **assists**, points, and game-winning goals.

Position: Right Wing
NHL Seasons: 17 (1971–1991)
Born: September 20, 1951, in Quebec, Canada

Position: Right Wing
NHL Seasons: 18 (1942–1960)
Born: August 4, 1921, in Montreal, Quebec, Canada

Maurice Richard

Maurice "Rocket" Richard played all of his 18 seasons with the Canadiens. The 14-time **All-Star** won the Hart Memorial Trophy as the most valuable player in 1947. The Rocket was well known for his intense and ultra-physical style of play. In addition to being a once-in-a-generation scorer, he was at the center of the Richard Riot scandal, in which 20,000 Montreal fans stormed the Montreal Forum in support of Richard, who felt that French-Canadian players were not being treated equally by referees.

Patrick Roy

Patrick Roy, nicknamed "Saint Patrick," played 20 seasons for the Canadiens and Colorado Avalanche during a career that led him into the Hall of Fame. He was selected to play in 17 All-Star games and won the Stanley Cup four times. Roy is widely considered to be the greatest goaltender in the history of the NHL, and is credited with completely changing the style of play for goalies. He was the first to successfully use the butterfly style, by which a goalie makes most saves from his knees. Today, many goalies use this style. Roy became the head coach of the Avalanche in the 2013–2014 season.

Position: Goaltender
NHL Seasons: 18 (1985–2003)
Born: October 5, 1965, in Quebec City, Quebec, Canada

Ken Dryden

Ken Dryden began his hockey career after graduating from prestigious Cornell University. He went on to have an impressive career beyond hockey as a lawyer, author, and eventually, as a member of parliament. Although his career as an NHL goalie was short, slightly more than seven seasons with the Canadiens, what he accomplished during those seven seasons is unmatched in NHL history. Dryden let up just 2.24 goals per game, won 258 games, and lost only 57. He also recorded 46 **shutouts** in just 397 games, shutting out the opposition in more than 10 percent of the games he played.

Position: Goaltender
NHL Seasons: 8 (1971–1979)
Born: August 8, 1947, in Hamilton, Ontario, Canada

Stars of Today

Today's Canadiens team is made up of many young, talented players who have proven that they are among the best in the league.

Carey Price

Carey Price began his NHL career in 2007 and was named to the NHL All-**Rookie** Team after recording a .920 **save percentage** with three shutouts that year. In 2008, in the playoffs against the Bruins, Price recorded a shutout, becoming the first Canadiens goalie to do so in the playoffs since Roy in 1986. Although he briefly lost his starting job in 2010, he came back strong, earning a place on the All-Star team in 2011 and cementing his position as the starting goalie. In the 2013–2014 season, Price showed his excellence, recording a career-best 2.32 **goals against average** and leading the Canadiens to a 100-point season.

Position: Goaltender
NHL Seasons: 8 (2007–Present)
Born: August 16, 1987, in Anahim Lake, British Columbia, Canada

Max Pacioretty

Chosen as the 22nd pick of the 2007 NHL **Entry Draft**, American left wing Max Pacioretty became the first Canadiens player to ever wear jersey number 67. In March 2011, Pacioretty was brutally hit by Bruins defenseman Zdeno Chara, suffering a back fracture and a severe concussion. The incident ended his season prematurely, but he has since fully recovered. In the 2013–2014 season, he scored 60 points and earned his first All-Star selection. The Canadiens expect to lean on Pacioretty as their most potent scorer in the 2014–2015 campaign.

Position: Left Wing
NHL Seasons: 7 (2008–Present)
Born: November 20, 1988, in New Canaan, Connecticut, USA

Tomas Plekanec

Tomas Plekanec is a talented playmaking center who excels at penalty killing. The Czech-born center was chosen 71st overall by the Canadiens in the 2001 NHL Entry Draft. Shortly after his second NHL season, Plekanec traveled to Latvia, where he helped the Czech Republic win a silver medal at the 2006 World Championships. Because of his great quickness and determination as a skater, Plekanec often helps on defense. The two-way player has skated for 11 seasons in the NHL, all of them with Montreal.

Position: Center
NHL Seasons: 11 (2003–Present)
Born: October 31, 1982, in Kladno, Czechoslovakia

P.K. Subban

P. K. Subban is an outstanding skater who has a unique ability to rush up the ice with the puck and recover with equal speed and anticipation. He can set up the offense on the **power play** and has a lethal **slap shot**. Subban is a physical defenseman who agitates opponents. During his five full NHL seasons, he has amassed nearly 170 points and has been named to two All-Star teams. Perhaps more significantly, he has helped anchor the young Canadiens defense and added to its reputation as a tough group.

Position: Defenseman
NHL Seasons: 6 (2009–Present)
Born: May 13, 1989, in Toronto, Ontario, Canada

All-Time Records

544
Most Career Goals
During his 18-season career with the Canadiens, Maurice "The Rocket" Richard scored 544 goals.

136
Most Points
In 1977, Guy Lafleur scored 136 points, setting the single-season Canadiens points record. He also holds the second, third, fourth, fifth, and sixth best single-season point records.

35
Division Titles
The Canadiens have won their division 35 times.

82
Most Assists
Peter Mahovlich had 82 assists in 1975, setting the club record.

1,256
Most Games
Henri Richard played in 1,256 games as a Canadien, more than any other player in the team's 105-year history.

Timeline

Throughout the team's history, the Canadiens have had many memorable events that have become defining moments for the team and its fans.

1909
On December 4, the Canadiens franchise begins. The NHL would not be founded for another eight years.

1956
Coach Toe Blake leads the team to win its first of five consecutive Stanley Cup Championships.

| 1900 | 1910 | 1920 | 1930 | 1940 | 1950 |

In 1931, the Canadiens finish with a record of 26-10-8 and win the division for the third time in four years. They go on to win the Stanley Cup, defeating the Chicago Blackhawks.

1916
The Canadiens win their first Stanley Cup after playing the Portland Rosebuds.

1944
After being a mediocre team for the previous 10 years, the Canadiens reestablish themselves by crushing the league on the way to a 38-5-7 record. They go on to win their first Cup in 13 seasons, once again beating the Blackhawks.

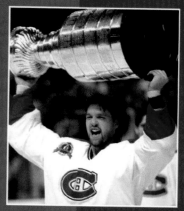

The Future

The Canadiens have a long history of winning. They have time and again proven to be the greatest franchise in the NHL, not only because they have won nearly 25 percent of all Stanley Cups, but because they have survived and thrived for 105 years. With a core group of young players to build on, the Canadiens have plenty of victories, and potentially even titles, ahead of them.

1993

The Stanley Cup celebrates 100 years of history, and fittingly, the oldest team in the league, the Canadiens, wins the Cup for the 24th time.

> In 1964, coach Frank Selke retires, and new general manager Sam Pollock joins the Canadiens. He leads the Canadiens to nine more Stanley Cup titles over the next 14 years.

| 1965 | 1975 | 1985 | 1995 | 2005 | 2015 |

1986

The Canadiens win their 23rd Stanley Cup against the Calgary Flames in the first all-Canadian Final since 1967. The team is led by head coach Jean Perron and goalie Patrick Roy, who was the youngest player to win the Conn Smythe Trophy as the MVP of the playoffs.

2008

The Canadiens defeat the Florida Panthers and become the first team to reach 3,000 victories. Their record of at least one Stanley Cup in nine consecutive decades ends in the 2000s.

Write a Biography

Life Story

A person's life story can be the subject of a book. This kind of book is called a biography. Biographies often describe the lives of people who have achieved great success. These people may be alive today, or they may have lived many years ago. Reading a biography can help you learn more about a great person.

Get the Facts

Use this book, and research in the library and on the internet, to find out more about your favorite Canadien. Learn as much about this player as you can. What position does he play? What are his statistics in important categories? Has he set any records? Also, be sure to write down key events in the person's life. What was his childhood like? What has he accomplished off the field? Is there anything else that makes this person special or unusual?

Use the Concept Web

A concept web is a useful research tool. Read the questions in the concept web on the following page. Answer the questions in your notebook. Your answers will help you write a biography.

Concept Web

Adulthood
- Where does this individual currently reside?
- Does he or she have a family?

Your Opinion
- What did you learn from the books you read in your research?
- Would you suggest these books to others?
- Was anything missing from these books?

Childhood
- Where and when was this person born?
- Describe his or her parents, siblings, and friends.
- Did this person grow up in unusual circumstances?

Write a Biography

Accomplishments off the Field
- What is this person's life's work?
- Has he or she received awards or recognition for accomplishments?
- How have this person's accomplishments served others?

Help and Obstacles
- Did this individual have a positive attitude?
- Did he or she receive help from others?
- Did this person have a mentor?
- Did this person face any hardships?
- If so, how were the hardships overcome?

Accomplishments on the Field
- What records does this person hold?
- What key games and plays have defined his career?
- What are his stats in categories important to his position?

Work and Preparation
- What was this person's education?
- What was his or her work experience?
- How does this person work?
- What is the process he or she uses?

Trivia Time

Take this quiz to test your knowledge of the Montreal Canadiens. The answers are printed upside down under each question.

1 How many Stanley Cups have the Canadiens won?

A. 24

2 How many coaches have the Canadiens had in team history?

A. 34

3 When was the last time the Canadiens won the Stanley Cup?

A. 1993

4 Which player is known as "Saint Patrick"?

A. Patrick Roy

5 What are the team colors of the Montreal Canadiens?

A. Red, blue, and white

6 What is the name of the Canadiens' arena?

A. The Bell Centre

7 Who had a picture of Ned Flanders on his helmet?

A. Peter Budaj

8 Which Canadiens coach holds the record for most wins in NHL history?

A. Scotty Bowman

9 Who is the current head coach of the Canadiens?

A. Michel Therrien

Key Words

All-Star: a game made for the best-ranked players in the NHL that happens mid-season. A player can be named an All-Star and then be sent to play in this game.

assists: a statistic that is attributed to up to two players of the scoring team who shoot, pass, or deflect the puck toward the scoring teammate

avatar: a figure that represents a person, especially in computer games or online

entry draft: an annual meeting where different teams in the NHL are allowed to pick new, young players who can join their teams

franchise: a team that is a member of a professional sports league

goals against average: a statistic that is the average of goals allowed per game by a goaltender

Great Depression: a long and difficult U.S. financial slump that began in 1929

logo: a symbol that stands for a team or organization

playoffs: a series of games that occur after regular season play

power play: when a player from one team is in the penalty box, the other team gains an advantage in the number of players

rookie: a player age 26 or younger who has played no more than 25 games in a previous season, nor six or more games in two previous seasons

save percentage: the rate at which a goalie stops shots being made toward his net by the opposing team

seed: a method of ranking teams for postseason play based on regular season records

shutouts: games in which the losing team is blocked from making any goals

slap shot: a hard shot made by raising the stick about waist high before striking the puck with a sharp slapping motion

Index

Log on to www.av2books.com

AV² by Weigl brings you media enhanced books that support active learning. Go to www.av2books.com, and enter the special code found on page 2 of this book. You will gain access to enriched and enhanced content that supplements and complements this book. Content includes video, audio, weblinks, quizzes, a slide show, and activities.

AV² Online Navigation

Audio
Listen to sections of the book read aloud.

Book Pages
AV² pages directly correspond to pages in the book.

Video
Watch informative video clips.

Embedded Weblinks
Gain additional information for research.

Key Words
Study vocabulary, and complete a matching word activity.

Try This!
Complete activities and hands-on experiments.

Quizzes
Test your knowledge.

Slide Show
View images and captions, and prepare a presentation.

AV² was built to bridge the gap between print and digital. We encourage you to tell us what you like and what you want to see in the future.

Sign up to be an AV² Ambassador at www.av2books.com/ambassador.

Due to the dynamic nature of the Internet, some of the URLs and activities provided as part of AV² by Weigl may have changed or ceased to exist. AV² by Weigl accepts no responsibility for any such changes. All media enhanced books are regularly monitored to update addresses and sites in a timely manner. Contact AV² by Weigl at 1-866-649-3445 or av2books@weigl.com with any questions, comments, or feedback.